CONTENT THAT SIZZLES AND SELLS

Create content that helps you build a magnetic and profitable personal brand.

GERTRUDE NONTERAH

Content that sizzles and sells:
create content that helps you build a magnetic and profitable personal
brand.

Printed by Amazon KDP Print

GeeNonterah.com

Acknowledgements

To my husband Fred Nonterah for unconditionally supporting my dreams.

CHAPTER 1

It started with a YouTube video on a cold Fall evening in 2012.

I was in graduate school, recently married and I was broke.

And so, I decided to look for cleaning gigs I could do over the weekend to catch up on some bills.

Then it happened.

I stumbled upon an interesting thing called *affiliate marketing.*

I did what most people my age do: I went to Google and typed in "what is affiliate marketing?"

That simple action has led to this book you're reading.

Why does this story matter? Here's why.

Long before I knew what content was, a woman called Lisa Irby had been blogging and creating videos on YouTube about making money online via her blogs and affiliate marketing.

On that afternoon back in 2012 when I was looking for extra ways to make money as a graduate student, Lisa's video, that she had made two or three years before taught me that even though my idea of cleaning homes over the weekend was a legit money-making path, I could start blogging and creating content from my home and make money as a result.

I became an instant fan!

I signed up for her email newsletter on her website.

I would later buy one of her online courses.

Since I watched that video, I have been able to generate six figures in online revenue from writing blog posts, creating videos, and freelance writing for other people. That money kept my bills paid when I suddenly lost my job as a postdoctoral biomedical researcher at the University of California San Diego in 2018.

What I've learned since that video allowed me to be there for my child with special needs when he needed me.

Lisa's video on affiliate marketing changed my life.

That's the power of content.

Lisa changed my life by educating me through her videos. In turn, she earned my admiration and money.

YOU CAN DO IT TOO

Never in the history of mankind has creating content been more accessible.

According to the data website Statista, as of November 2020, 4.66 billion people have access to the internet. That is 59% of the world's population.

This means that one in every two individuals on planet Earth -

whether they are using a cell phone, a tablet, or a computer; or whether that internet is lightning fast or moves at a slow pace - has access to the internet.

That is a staggering statistic that provides you and me with a lot of opportunity.

I follow people from Ghana, Kenya, Nigeria, The Philippines, Armenia, and England, just to name a few, who create helpful content and who are compensated very well as a result. It doesn't matter if this content is on Instagram, LinkedIn, YouTube, through blog posts, or via a podcast.

Regardless of where you are from, your educational status, or your socioeconomic status, it is possible right now to build a profitable personal brand using content.

In this book, you'll learn how.

WHO THIS BOOK IS FOR

If you picked up this book, then I assume that you are ready to build a magnetic personal brand that makes you money.

Before we go any further, let's talk about who this book is *not* for.

This book is not for you if:

1. You think you can do everything in this book in a day and magically get results.

2. You think you will start today and make bucket loads of cash tomorrow.
3. You like to complain and blame your problems on other people.
4. You think you don't have to work hard for what you deserve.
5. You criticize people who are successful even though they have worked hard to get where they are.

If any of the above describes you, please close the pages of this book, and pretend you never saw it.

Nobody will ever know.

Still here? Alright! Let's get this going.

This book is for you if you'd like to learn how to build a magnetic and profitable personal brand using content.

At this point, you might have noticed that I have mentioned the phrase "personal brand" a few times. So let's define it before we move further.

A personal brand involves leveraging your personality, your gifts, experiences, and your abilities to become well-known in a particular industry.

You can build a personal brand both as an employee who clocks in and out of a job *and* as an entrepreneur.

As someone who has benefitted from building a personal brand, I can tell you, having a personal brand has paid off in ways I never expected. It has landed me in places I once dreamed of.

Building a personal brand has led to:

- Landing my current role as a science writer with an agency that serves larger-than-life life science companies like Pfizer and Thermo Fisher Scientific
- Sales of my digital products
- A number 1 Amazon new release book
- Invitations to be interviewed on podcasts
- Invitations to speak at events including at renowned universities
- Opportunities to work with brands in a paid capacity.

Building a personal brand has paid off.

Before we move on, let me address one of the biggest misconceptions of building a personal brand which is that, in order to be successful you need a large following on social media or that you need to become a celebrity-like figure.

This is not true.

I have been able to accomplish the above with a total online following of fewer than 10,000 followers across *all* the platforms I am active on.

I am hardly an influencer.

But by creating content that helped other people with their goals and problems, I've been able to leverage that personal brand profitably.

WHY YOU SHOULD START CREATING CONTENT NOW

Your content has a worldwide reach. When you post anything on the internet, it is possible that people from countries you have never heard of or never thought existed will find you. The implications here are wild! For instance, there are businesses in other countries that I have only ever encountered online because their content is so good. Their content is so good that I tend to take note of such businesses so that if I ever visit those countries, I will go and support them. So if you have a business that is local and you create content that reaches a worldwide audience, if you are consistent and telling a compelling story (more on that later), they will patronize your business.

You don't have to stick to one mode of content creation. You can create videos, audio content, post pictures, or write a blog. Another powerful thing about multiple modes of content like this is the fact that if you don't like one mode, you can move on to something else! If you don't like video, try creating audio content. Hate audio? Try written content. There is room for everyone in the world of content creation.

Your content can serve different purposes in your business. You may decide to create content to promote a local business you already have. A great example of this is the story of Roger Wakefield. Roger owns a plumbing business in Texas. The marketing company he had hired to help get customers in the door for the business charged his company a premium price but whatever they were doing, was not bringing customers through the door. So Roger learned all he could about creating videos on YouTube - because it intrigued him. Roger started posting videos in 2017. It is November 2020 as I am writing this and Roger has 200,000 subscribers on his channel, over 17 million views and because of how well he positioned himself using his content, his company does not have to worry about business coming in every day! Other plumbers may have to worry about people calling in to book appointments - but not Roger! Creating videos on YouTube allowed him to market his business to the tune of a few million dollars, on a free platform. Popular online entrepreneur personality Gary Vee talks about using video to promote his father's wine shop. Gwen Addo, a Ghanaian entrepreneur sells hair extensions internationally from her shop in Accra, Ghana by leveraging content on Instagram.

You can create content to promote an online/virtual business. If you have an e-commerce business that sells widgets online, you can use content to promote that. You can also use content to promote:

- online courses
- your books
- your speaking
- coaching/consulting packages

You can also create content *as your business*. It is possible to create content and use that to make money. This is how influencers make money. They create content and make money as a result. That could look like this:

- Getting paid by companies to do sponsored content
- Using a monetizable platform like YouTube to get paid through ads

Content establishes you as an authority in your field. Sometime in 2019, I decided to focus on talking about writing for a living on my YouTube channel. Since then, I have talked about freelance writing, writing books, and blogging. As a result of this, I have had people request for me to coach them to write their books. And even though I've never enjoyed the word "guru", recently one of my online business friends called me a "writing guru". If you talk genuinely and authoritatively about a subject enough, you will become an expert in that area. You may not be the foremost expert, but sharing your experience counts and people value it.

Content will set you apart. While it may seem like the world is drowning in a sea of content, the truth is that 90% of content on the internet is mediocre. I know somebody may come at me for that, but this is true! There are a lot of people who start but never continue. There are those who create a great video today and won't create another for 6 months. Between inconsistent content, people who start and fizzle out almost immediately, and just plain bad content, there is MORE than enough room for you to shine in your path if you decide to do things differently. We will talk more about that in a later chapter.

Here's the bottom-line - *content is powerful*. Creating the right content will help you grow into the brand people want to work with and buy from. In this book, we will go over exactly how to create that type of content that sizzles and sells. But first, let's bust some myths.

CHAPTER 2

CONTENT MYTHS TO STOP BELIEVING RIGHT NOW

You need hundreds of followers to make content work for you.

Having hundreds or even thousands of followers on any platform is impressive. Psychology and sociology tell us that humans automatically associate authority with larger numbers. Thus, there is a natural tendency to trust the numbers. If we have to choose between two restaurants, we might choose the one that has 500 reviews rather than the one with 20. When we see somebody has 100,000 Twitter followers we are immediately intrigued and want to find out why so many people follow this person's opinions. This concept of "social proof" plays out in various life scenarios. It is natural to think the person with 250,000 subscribers on YouTube has more credibility compared to the other person covering the same subject matter with 2,000 subscribers.

But this is not always true.

While larger numbers are impressive and may allow you to reach more people, it is better to have a smaller audience or following who is engaged than a large number who hardly care about your message, brand or business.

A trend that has become increasingly common online is for people to "buy followers".

No matter how tempting it may seem, please avoid this.

Buying followers will dilute your message, make your marketing appear ineffective and because consumers are savvier these days, they will be able to see right through it.

I'll reiterate - you are better off with 1000 followers who truly enjoy your content and are more likely to patronize your services, than 10,000 followers who do not care or worse, are not even real.

You need to create and share content 10 times a day.

I was at a meeting one day when a lady told me she had been following an Instagram guru online who was teaching that in order to be successful on the platform, you had to post 3 times a day.

This advice was stressing her out because she did not know how to create that many pieces of content per day.

Listen, I get where "create 200 pieces of content per day" may come from.

When I first got online and got active on social media in the early 2010's, this advice was common. This was when social media platforms showed your content to people in a chronological manner. Thus, by publishing multiple times a day, the idea was that you would capture multiple people online at different times of the day.

I remember one social media educator who used to post 10 times a day!

Social media platforms don't work that way anymore.

They are based on complicated algorithms that reward publishers like you for the engagement your posts receive. And most of the time, this is regardless of when you posted that content.

Thus, trying to ride the hamster wheel of frantic content creation will not just wear you out, it will make you want to quit.

When people talk to me about social media content creation, here is the advice I give them: it is better to create one meaningful piece of content than to create 20 pieces that are utterly useless.

Don't post meaningless content. It makes you look less credible than you really are.

Creating and posting content does not have to be stressful. Later on in the book, we will talk about what I mean by "meaningful" content.

The kind of content working for your competitor will work for you

Emulation is definitely the best kind of flattery. And I think there should be people who you want to emulate as a content creator. The best artists "steal" anyway! There is no truly original idea. Having said that however, it is important to realize that what works for one content creator will not necessarily work for you.

Here is why.

It is important to know several things about the audience you are creating content for. In understanding your audience, you will have to gather demographic information.

According to National Geographic, demography (the word from which we derive demographics) is the study of human populations.

This includes:

- Age range
- Ethnicity or cultural background
- Language
- Gender
- How much money this group earns
- Where they live in the world
- The types of neighborhoods they may live in, in

that part of the world

- Educational status (e.g., you might talk differently to people who have PhDs in anthropology than you would talk to high school students)

All of these pieces of information are important to content creators. Knowing as many of these as possible is key to your success as a content creator.

In addition to pinpointing the demographics of the audience you are creating for, you have to be tuned in to their psychographics. Psychographics taps into the attitudes, values, desires and ways of thinking for a population. For instance, if you create marriage content - the way most people in Ghana, the country where I grew up - think about marriage is going to be vastly different from the way a typical American of the same age may think about marriage. Thus in creating that type of content, you will have to take that into consideration.

Now, the danger in emulating someone else's content is that while their style of content could work for you, chances are it won't because the demographics and psychographics of their audience could be completely different from the people *you* are trying to reach.

Thus whereas they might post something and get tons of engagement, you may do something similar and see it fall flat.

Learning the specific demographic and psychographic information for your audience is not a cake-walk. It can take years to really dial it in. But as the old adage goes, "Rome was not built in a day". You have to start somewhere. We will talk about how you can start learning about the demographics and psychographics of the people who will consume your content later on in the book.

You can throw anything up on the internet and people will find it
No! This is not true.

The days of expecting people to find you simply because you now "own" a tiny bit of the internet are gone.

When I started writing on Yahoo Geocities (you might be able to tell my age by this reference alone), it was true that publishing anything on the internet would get you attention. However, with the growth of the internet has come the growth of users. Internet users now have many more choices to pay attention to.

These days, you have to *earn* attention.

So while creating content is an important piece to the puzzle, making it stand out is crucial.

Random acts of content
This one is not a myth as much as it is a piece of advice that I

want to mention before we move on.

Even though I am not an advocate for posting 20 random pieces of content instead of one meaningful one, it is also important to stay consistent with your content creation process.

If you only blog once in 6 months and hardly do any blog promotion, you cannot say creating content doesn't work.

It is important to be committed to the process.

I like how YouTube creator and online business owner Sean Cannell puts it, "create one impactful piece of content each week".

Stress-free consistency that works for your business goals is the name of the game.

CHAPTER 3

IT IS ABOUT THEM, NOT YOU - THE POWER OF STORY

Your content is about the audience you serve - not you.

Yes, you may be the one creating the videos and you may be the one creating the audios for the podcast. But ultimately, your content is not for you or about you. It is about the people you want to attract to your brand, message, or business.

In the book *Building A Story Brand,* author Donald Miller talks at length about this.

This is a book on how to create content that sizzles and sells. In order to effectively sell, you have to know the story of your audience.

The story of your audience
I want you to think about your favorite movie.

One of my favorite all-time movies is *Legally Blonde*.

In the movie, Elle Woods, a rich socialite from California is dumped by her boyfriend who is off to Harvard Law School and thus needs someone who is "more serious".

Elle, played by Reese Witherspoon, is a stereotypical sorority party girl with "blonde hair and big boobs" and according to this foolish boyfriend, this would be a mismatch for his goals.

I am rolling my eyes as I write this.

The long and short of it is that Elle decides that she is going to get her boyfriend back by working hard to pass the law school entrance exam and getting into Harvard.

On her first day, after being embarrassed by a professor, Elle meets a third-year law student who becomes her guide throughout the rest of the movie.

In the end, Elle argues the case of a murder suspect and wins the case.

Of course, by this point, we all see what a fool the ex-boyfriend is. I am elated each time I watch one of the scenes at the end of the film where Elle dumps him after he tries to come back!

It makes for a good Friday movie with popcorn.

But we're not talking about calories here.

We are talking specifically about the structure of every good tale that has been told from the beginning of time.

We usually start with our hero of the story.

The story is introduced to us at a point when the hero faces a dilemma - a problem of some kind. That problem could be physical, emotional, psychological, or spiritual.

We then watch the hero try to solve that dilemma.

In every good story, on the hero's way to solving that dilemma, they meet a guide - it could be a person or a book or even a song - that guides them through the dilemma including around all the obstacles they encounter on the way to solving the problem.

By the end of the movie, the dilemma is resolved and you and I can let out a sigh of relief!

No matter the genre, every good story follows this format.

In *Legally Blonde,* this is how that breaks down.

Hero: Elle is the hero.
The dilemma: Her dilemma is that her boyfriend has left her and she is trying to get him back. This will involve her going to the same law school as him: Harvard Law.
The Guide: After she meets her first obstacle, a snarky professor who embarrasses her, she meets a guide to help her not give up on Harvard Law. The guide is with her through the movie.
The Resolution: Elle defends a high-profile case and wins. Because of this, her ex tries to make a comeback. But by the end of the movie, she realizes that the boyfriend was a fool anyway and so she says no to his request.

Why is this important?

It is important because this is exactly how to create meaningful content that sizzles and gets people to buy from you.

In your business, you have to realize that *your potential customer is the hero*. The audience you are building and nurturing, are the heroes. Their dilemma is whichever problem your business solves for them.

If you're a plumber - the dilemma is that clogged toilet that is overflowing.

If you're a hairdresser - the dilemma is unpresentable hair for your hero's all-important interview.

If you're a mental health counselor - the dilemma is the crisis your hero is going through because they recently lost a loved one and are not sure how to move on in their lives.

Now for a harsh truth.

Your potential clients and customers DO NOT care about you. This sounds harsh, but it is true. The people who will buy from you - the hero - do not care if your business was founded in 1850 or if it started in 2019. The hero does not care about the awards you have won. The hero hardly cares about what you ate for breakfast or lunch. And they definitely do not care about your logo (I could go on and on about businesses wasting time on logos when they should be focused on sales, but this is NOT the book for that.)

I'm not saying these things are not important or don't provide credibility to your business.

What I am saying is that, on the hierarchy of needs as far as your hero is concerned, these aspects are not at the top.

They may appreciate these later on, but in the moment when they are going through the dilemma, all they want is to solve that problem; to get rid of the pain.

Thus, it is important in your content creation process to think about the exact dilemma your ideal client or customer is facing. Please don't leave this out of your business processes and definitely do not leave it out of your content creation process.

The best way to know the dilemma your hero is facing is to ask them.

It is so simple that even I forget it sometimes.

Ask the people you are creating content for.

Yes in the beginning when you have 10 or 20 people reading your blog or listening to your podcast, you may not get a lot of responses back.

But even with the smallest audience, you will always find one person who will give you information that will provide insight into what their dilemma is.

For instance, when I started blogging, I was not getting anywhere.

There were a few hundred people reading my blog but there wasn't anything wild about it. And then I began to ask the people who had signed up for my email list for feedback. This helped me to focus on topics that mattered to the audience I was serving. This then guided the digital products I created and now guides my coaching and even the topics I get invited to speak on.

If you want to create the type of content that resonates with your audience and moves them to make buying decisions, you must ask them. Find out what their dilemma is and create content that answers *that*.

Here are seven powerful ways to find out your hero's dilemma.

When you are brand new

#1- Remember when I said you don't want to copy other people's content? This still holds. However, you can still get an idea of the dilemmas your heroes are facing by reading the comments of other content creators. Let's say you have a hairdressing business, and you want to start creating content around that. One of the gifts you can give yourself is to find other hairdressers who have content online. This could be a YouTube channel, an Instagram or Facebook page, a blog, or a podcast. Go "listen" to what people are saying on those pieces of content. I recommend you get a notebook - physical or virtual - and write down those comments and questions. If you are new to creating content and have no idea where to start, this is what I recommend. Start here and refine as your audience grows.

#2 - Another way to identify your hero's dilemma is to visit online forums and groups. Facebook groups have been a great source of digging into the dilemma of my hero in the past. Facebook communities exist for every imaginable topic under the sun. If you absolutely refuse to use Facebook, then try online forums. You can find these forums by typing the subject topic and the word "forums" into Google. Reddit is another powerful place for you to gain a sense of your hero's dilemma.

#3 - I have recently come to love Quora, which is a question and answer website. This is another place to learn the dilemma of your hero. You will find your heroes asking questions here that you can answer with your content.

#4 - Amazon reviews. Even if you never plan to sell on Amazon, reading Amazon reviews will be helpful for you. Five-star reviews don't always give you the whole picture. When you read 4-star and 3-star reviews, however, you get to understand why or how people were unsatisfied with that particular product.

When you have built a following (no matter how small)

#5 - Send out surveys. This works best when you have already built an audience. You can create surveys with Google Forms or the free version of Survey Monkey.

#6 - Listen to the comments and feedback they leave on the content you have created. Your heroes will leave you questions and comments that you can turn into content. They may also ask you questions in person. Take note of those! As a content creator, get into the habit of listening to unsolicited, *constructive* feedback.

#7 - Get on the phone! I am not a big fan of phone calls but you learn a lot when you talk to people. Most of the time, you will be creating content that reaches people all over the world and so it might not be feasible to meet in person. You can get on a phone or use voice-over-internet-protocol services like Zoom and Skype to communicate. I recommend recording such calls because they will use specific words and language that you want to take note of. You want to take note of the language because you want to use that exact language when you create your content. More on that later!

You are the guide

Your customer is the hero and you are the guide.

Businesses that position themselves as the hero tend to lose their potential clients and customers with their content because they don't speak their language.

Don't make this mistake!

Your potential client or customer is on their own journey with their own dilemma and until you can show them that you *care* about that dilemma, everything you create will sound like noise.

So like the third-year law student in *Legally Blonde* who becomes Elle's guide, you will come alongside that customer or client and use your content to help them get to a resolution.

That means for the hairdresser, you come alongside that girl who wants to have the perfect hair-do for her interview and say "We got this, I am going to help you look good for that interview."

When customers and clients see that you are on their side and that you want them to win through your content, that is how you begin to convince them to buy. Furthermore, because you have helped these individuals reach the resolution in their story, they will become *superfans* (a term coined by online entrepreneur Pat Flynn, which is also the title of his book) who recommend your business to everyone.

If you begin to think about your content as the help you are providing your potential client or customer as they resolve their dilemma, you will sell more with your content.

"But what about the creator's story?"

You can absolutely use your story in your content creation process.

In my book *Win At Freelance Writing,* I tell the story of how losing my job as a postdoctoral fellow at University of California San Diego, led me to start my own freelance writing business.

People love to hear your "origin story". This is why you might ask someone, "so what do you do?" or "where are you from?" when you first meet them.

We humans are curious beings.

But usually, we don't care about that information until it benefits us.

Let me prove that to you.

You are at a networking event and you meet some new people and so you decide to strike a conversation with some of them. Your questions "what do you do?" and "where are you from?" are genuine, and you might learn some interesting information by asking those questions.

Using that information, you may single out one or two people who you find interesting and who you might want to continue a conversation with because what they do is directly linked with your goals. So while you might be interested in the different stories you might hear during that event, you might come away with *one* connection that was especially meaningful to you.

We are more inclined to align ourselves with people who can help us in some way.

There's a popular quote by Zig Ziglar that says, "you can have everything you want in life if you will just help enough other people get what they want".

If you show your potential clients and customers that you care about their dilemma and are on a quest to solve it, first, they will in turn care about *your story*.

So yes, weave in the fact that you have been around for 100 years and share pictures of your cat.

But let it be tied to what your audience needs and wants.

CHAPTER 4

THE THREE MAJOR TYPES OF CONTENT

While there are hundreds of content types you could create, you can essentially break those content types into 3 groups.

1. Written content - This includes blog posts, text-only social media posts, white papers, eBooks, brochures, product descriptions, emails.

2. Video and visual content - You can create videos on Facebook, Instagram, LinkedIn, Twitter, YouTube and Twitch. On many of these platforms you can create short-form "stories" that are usually about 15 seconds long. You have a choice of pre-recorded video or live video. Webinars are a popular video content type that online marketers use to sell. Visual platforms like Pinterest and Instagram focus on users posting eye-catching images. Photographs and infographics are examples of visual content.

3. Audio content - Podcasts and radio shows are the major way people consume audio content.

I lay out the three types of content because I usually

encounter people who think they have to do it all.

I am here to announce and affirm that you certainly, absolutely, do not have to create all the different types of content out there.

Trying to do it all is overwhelming and you'll fizzle out if you don't have a large team to create all that content.

What I recommend instead is that you choose two main content platforms that you can focus on.

For instance, as of this writing, I focus my content creation efforts on YouTube and Instagram.

I do have a blog that is related to my YouTube channel, but in this season, I am focused on growing an audience I can serve on YouTube and Instagram.

I also have LinkedIn. And I have had a podcast.

But because I am a team of one (with the occasional help of a contractor), it is important that I focus my energies on a few things rather than be spread out.

Here's an example of focusing on two content platforms could look like.

Joe owns a local coffee shop and he would like to start creating sizzling content so he can get more people into his shop.

Let's also say he has done his research and found out that most of his customers are mostly ages 25-40 who stop by his shop on their daily commute.

Joe could start a podcast called "Crazy Commute Stories" where he showcases the anonymous tales of commuters who come through his shop.

To get these stories, he could ask his customers as they wait on their brew, "what is your craziest commute story?"

He could then take one of those stories each week (with permission) and talk about it for 10-15 minutes on a podcast. And of course, because it is his show, Joe is also going to be able to plug in invitations for a cup of coffee at his shop.

A second platform I would then recommend for Joe is Instagram - because of the demographic he serves.

He can then use user-generated content on his page by asking his customers to use a special hashtag to get featured on the official coffee shop page.

Does this mean Joe can never create content on any other platforms?

No.

It just means he will focus on mastering the two platforms he has chosen - his podcast and Instagram page, before he moves on to other platforms.

This key is so important and I have personally made the mistake of thinking I could be everywhere.

Every time you are tempted to create on multiple content

platforms when you haven't mastered at least one, I want you to remind yourself of this proverb, "A man who chases two rabbits, catches none".

Content marketing - or using your content to market your business - is effective. But it is only effective if you execute effectively. And one of those ways is to focus on just a few platforms - I recommend two - rather than spreading yourself thin.

EXERCISE - In this chapter, you learned about the three major types of content you can create for your business.

- Written content
- Video and Visual content
- Audio content

And you can create this content on multiple platforms.

I am an advocate for choosing a main platform and a secondary platform that will be an "outpost" of sorts. This second platform is not the main platform most people encounter you on but it is very important in your content strategy.

The main platform - This platform will house your longer

form content. This will usually be a blog, podcast or YouTube channel. With the main platform, people encounter you for a longer period of time and it tends to be the one where you will have most people following you. On this platform, creating one piece of long-form content per week is a good place to start.

The outpost platform - Remember, this platform is just as important as the first one! However, this is where you will create shorter form content. And because those content pieces are shorter, you are able to create multiple pieces of content per week. Good examples of outpost platforms are Twitter, Instagram, LinkedIn and Facebook.

So for instance, you might choose to have a blog as your main platform and use Twitter as your outpost to share your blog content.

Or in Joe the coffee shop owner's example, you can choose to have a weekly podcast and then use Instagram as your outpost platform.

So based on what you've learned so far, get a notebook and write down, two content platforms you are confident you can stay consistent with.

CHAPTER 5

CONTENT RULES TO FOLLOW

Every game has rules and so does content creation. Just like every story has a hero who faces a dilemma and then seeks a resolution of that dilemma, your content must follow certain rules or else it will fall flat.

And we don't want that!

In this chapter, we will talk about key content rules you should follow if you want your content marketing to be effective.

But before we jump into talking about that, let's talk about a term that may (or may not) be new to you.

Content marketing: what is it?

According to Hubspot, "content marketing is the process of planning, creating, distributing, sharing, and publishing content to reach your target audience. It can boost factors like brand awareness, sales, reach, interactions, and loyalty."

Let's take that line by line.

"the process of planning, creating, distributing, sharing and publishing content"
As you can see from this part of the definition, content marketing is a multi-step process that involves:

- planning
- creating
- distributing/sharing
- publishing

This means you have to have a strategy. Like I mentioned earlier in the book, you cannot expect to be haphazard with your content marketing and expect it to work.

You have to plan what you want to create. You will then create it. And then after you have published it, you will have to share and distribute it (yes, you can even recruit your audience to help you do this).

Thus, it is important to have a content strategy. More on that in a minute.

"...to reach your target audience"

You are not creating content for everybody.

It is tempting to want to include everyone in your content marketing strategy.

But a popular marketing adage is, "if you try to reach everyone, you reach no-one".

Earlier on, we talked about delving into the demographics and psychographics of your audience.

Before you start doing anything, please revisit and review chapter 3. Going through that chapter will help you narrow down who you want to reach with your content.

"It can boost factors like brand awareness, sales, reach, interactions, and loyalty."

This is the part most business owners think about and rightly so! However, in order for brand awareness, sales, reach, interactions and loyalty to happen, the first two things need to happen.

- You should know your target audience
- You should have a content strategy

Since we've already talked about how to investigate your audience, let's now talk about having a content strategy that follows the rules.

RULE #1-Your content should ALWAYS answer these two questions

Even if it is a simple 280-word tweet, every piece of content you create should have the two goals.

1. A goal for *your* business. How is the piece of content you're creating tie into your marketing plan for your business? Is this piece of content meant to drive awareness or to make sales? Are you trying to get them on your email list for a

webinar? Before you publish any piece of content, there should be a clear goal for that piece of content. Even if you make fun little videos and share hilarious memes, it should benefit your business somehow.

2. The second question (or goal) is to ask "how will this benefit my audience?" What will your readers, listeners or followers gain from consuming the content you're about to publish? Will they be educated? Will they be entertained? Will it change their life in some way?

A great example of content marketing that fits this thought is from blogger Amanda Rettke of Iambaker.net.

Amanda has been blogging about deserts since 2008 and has been featured on the *Today Show* and *Oprah*.

Well, I did not know about Amanda until I stumbled upon one of her hilarious Instagram Reels.

In an Instagram Reel series she dubbed "Your Content Is Terrible", Amanda plays a customer service character called Shirley who takes calls from people who are dissatisfied with bad content online and hilariously files reports on their behalf.

At first, people thought it was weird that she was posting funny videos instead of focusing on posting pictures of her delicious desserts.

But here is what happened instead - although people came for Amanda aka Shirley's jokes, they stayed for her dessert recipes.

Comments like "This is getting me through a tough time" show how Amanda's funny content is reaching people during a tough time. On Amanda's @iambaker Instagram page, her hilarious Reels are interspersed with pictures of her dessert recipes.

Genius!

And so even in posting what seemed like funny and unrelated content, Amanda was able to attract people to find her recipes because she created content that clearly had a goal.

I am not saying go out there and start posting funny content just to gain attention. It has to be in context - in Amanda's case it was and it ended up working very well for her.

However, this is an example of how even what looks like random content can serve both you and your audience.

THE GOAL CANNOT BE RANDOM

Making funny videos that attract people to find your product and services is fine.

But doing this has to be strategic.

I believe there is content that you can do for pure educational or entertainment value but, it is important to beware of creating too much of that type of content.

When I first started blogging in 2012, I did a lot of this.

I was naïve back then and thought by creating "helpful" and "value-packed" content, I would automatically attract people who wanted to patronize my products and services. Based on this experience, I would say that this is where most content creators fail.

It is fine to create helpful and value-packed content.

In fact, with all the competition online these days, you should!

But, unless you make that content to solve a specific problem in the life of your ideal client or customer which then will lead you to offer them a product or service that helps them even further, that content could be a waste of your time.

Here's what I mean.

About seven years ago, I gave birth to my son.

I had gone to the hospital for a routine check-up when the physician noticed that my blood pressure was high - a condition called preeclampsia - and so they would have to deliver my baby two weeks early.

At first, I was like "Oh okay, we are about to meet our baby!"

My husband and I were a little anxious but not too worried.

In situations like mine, doctors will give women a hormone called oxytocin to get the contractions going so they can deliver. So that is what they did.

About six hours later though, I was in the worst pain of my life! I cried so much the nurse had to take off the oxygen mask I was wearing and pour my tears in a sink!

This was the only time I had cried enough for the tears to be poured into a sink!

So imagine my relief when another doctor showed up and asked me if I wanted an epidural, a type of anesthesia that reduces the pain?

The big needle the doctor stuck in my back to give me the epidural did not matter. I was in a world of pain. I was going to take *anything* that made the pain go away. I wanted the pain to go away so I could have that baby safely and we could be a happy family.

Similarly, you have people in your audience who have a pain they need desperately to go away.

Let's take weight loss.

Shelly wants to lose weight. But her deeper reason for losing weight is that she has been struggling to get pregnant and losing some of the weight will increase those chances. She is not trying to lose weight to be vain. This weight loss journey means something deeper to her than just looks - nothing wrong with looks - but she wants more than that.

So in this case, it will not be enough to post a workout video.

On the other hand, a workout video that also speaks to the pain of trying to get pregnant but not being able to because of your weight, will connect with that person and increase the chances that they engage your content and buy whatever it is that you offer.

And this is why knowing and being in tune with the psychographics of your audience is so crucial.

When you create content with the deep pains of your audience in mind, you're more likely to connect with them and ultimately, convert them to become paying customers.

ACTIVITY

Revisit the chapter 3. Make it a habit to talk to your audience at least once in every three months to learn how best you can solve their problems both with free content and with your products and services.

RULE #2- Include stories, data and examples
Including data and examples in your content is powerful.

So far, in this book, I have given you several examples and I just shared a bit of my birth story as an analogy!

Whether you are creating audio, video or written content, including stories, data and examples, is a powerful way to draw people in and keep them reading.

Yes, people want you to give them the facts, but I want you to think about your favorite teacher from any level of your educational experience.

Chances are that they are the teacher that told you crazy stories and who always gave examples that made it easier to understand the information.

Same idea here! Let's talk about how to use each in your content.

Stories
No matter how boring you think your life is, you have stories to tell.

Think through your life experiences:

- Your family life
- School life
- Friendships/relationships
- Travels
- Something you observed
- A major life event such as the birth of a child, loss of a family member or an accident

Back when I sold a digital product on how to become a social media manager, I told the story of how moving to a new expensive city forced me to level up and start a profitable side hustle.

This story resonated with my audience and I ended up selling a few thousand dollars worth of the book. It's how some people became loyal fans of my brand.

A powerful story I read about when I was starting my blogging journey is from super-blogger Jon Morrow. Jon has made millions of dollars from his blog - from his wheelchair.

Here's a snippet of his story in his own words from an article called **"On Dying, Mothers and Fighting for your ideas"**.

> "The doctor cleared his throat. "I'm sorry, but I have bad news."
>
> He paused, looking down at the floor. He looked back up at her. He started to say something and then stopped, looking back down at the floor.
>
> That's when Pat began to cry.
>
> She'd argued with herself about even coming to the doctor's office. Her baby was a year old, and he hadn't started crawling yet. He tried, yes, dragging his legs behind him as he struggled to make it just a few feet on the floor, but it didn't look right. Everyone told her that she was worrying over nothing, and maybe she was, but she told herself that she would take him to the

doctor, just to be safe …

"Your son has a neuromuscular disorder called Spinal Muscular Atrophy," the doctor said. "It's a form of muscular dystrophy that primarily affects children."

Pat was speechless. Everyone had told her she was silly. She had hoped she was wrong, prayed she was wrong, but still . . . she knew.

"What's going to happen to him?" she managed to say.

"Where most children grow stronger as they get older, your son is going to get weaker. He'll lose the ability to move. He'll lose the ability to breathe on his own. And one day, he'll catch an infection that will spread into his respiratory system, giving him severe pneumonia …"

She held up her hand to stop him. "You're saying he is going to die?"

He nodded. "There are three types of SMA. Caught this early, your son almost certainly has Type I. Most children with Type I die of pneumonia before the age of two." He paused. "I'm sorry."

Pat looked up into his face and saw that he really was sorry. It made her angry. Not because of his pity, but because in this man's eyes, her baby was already dead.

"Don't be sorry," Pat said, wiping tears away from her face. Her voice was suddenly very calm. "He isn't going to die."

"It's important you understand the situation, Mrs. Morrow. The pneumonia … he won't be able to fight it."

"He won't have to," she said. "I'll fight it for him."

Read the whole post here - https://copyblogger.com/fight-for-your-ideas/

Did you feel the tension? Could you feel the frustration of Mrs Morrow's sense of despair and that turn in her emotions that helped her fight through something that was supposed to kill her child by the time he was two?

That is the power of storytelling.

This is one of those stories I go back to from time to time when I need inspiration as a blogger and writer. You can do the same with your content. You can share as much or as little as you want of your story or any story for that matter.

The point here is this: stories are powerful and while people may forget the hard facts, they usually will remember the stories. If you are able to weave it well into your content that also addresses the pain of your ideal clients, your content will always land well.

Data
Because of my background in biomedical research, I am a stickler for finding data sources from an original piece of

research. Even when I find statistics quoted on a reputable website, I dig through the references they have cited to make sure those are the right numbers.

Where to find relevant data to quote in your content.

Finding data that supports your content adds a layer of credibility to your content. Don't ignore it.

My word of caution here however, is to always use reliable sources when you cite a piece of data. This is why I mentioned above that even if I find a statistic on a popular website like WebMD or Healthline or a news website, I dig to find the source of that data.

Fact-checking as a content creator is important. As a content creator, you are building trust with the people who consume your content. Quoting the wrong data can make you lose that trust.

Here are a handful of websites where you can find reliable/research-backed data sources.

PubMed.gov - PubMed is a website that is managed by the United States National Library of Medicine. It contains a collection of original research articles, reviews and meta analyses that stretch as far back as the early 1900s.

PubMed is free to use and will usually serve up abstracts - a type of scientific summary - of these research articles.

In some instances, you can access the full-length articles while you can only access abstracts for some of the articles.

Nonetheless, it is a rich source of health and science-related data.

Google Scholar - Google Scholar is hosted by Google and does something similar to PubMed. I have a few colleagues who think Google Scholar is better than PubMed.

Google Scholar like PubMed will serve up research articles around a subject when you do a search for a specific term.

USA.gov - USA.gov is another US-based government website where you can find US-related facts to cite in your content.

The CIA World Factbook - The CIA World Factbook does a good job of providing data on countries. If you need to find data or information about a country, this is a good resource.

Gallup - Gallup has been a long time leader in providing poll information and statistics. They have years of statistics and data you can use.

Statista - According to the Statista website, you can "find statistics, consumer survey results and industry studies from over 22500 sources on over 60000 topics on the internet's leading statistics database."

If you need to quote data consumer behavior and the market, Statista is the place to go and find that data.

Between these six websites, you can find a wealth of data and information to quote to make your content look more credible and to increase trust.

Whether you create video content, audio content, written content or you primarily create images on Instagram, your brand and business will benefit from including data to your content creation process.

Examples and analogies

Initially, I was going to include this under the stories section and then I realized "nope, this deserves it's own section!"

I am an adjunct professor of biology at a college in the San Diego area. Biology is not an easy subject to study. I was a Biology major myself in college and I can attest to this fact. Thus, one of the tools I love to use as a teacher is to provide my students with examples and analogies.

No matter how complex the idea is, if I am able to find an analogy or example that illustrates my point, I increase the chances that my students will remember.

For most people, unless there is an example or analogy we can visualize, concepts are hard to grasp.

At the end of each class where I used an excellent analogy to describe something, students thank me for giving them something to remember the content. So take it from me when I say that examples and analogies will make your content memorable.

How does one come up with analogies and examples though?

Personally, I think it comes from years of knowing your subject. It comes from years of reading, listening to new developments in your industry and practicing your craft.

Now, if you are new to the industry you are trying to create content in, don't worry!

You can still give great examples and analogies.

If you read wide, you will come up with examples and analogies to use in your content. I love to listen to audiobooks when I exercise. I also listen to a lot of podcasts. If there is an example or analogy I hear that I like, I mentally file it away for a rainy day.

You can even create your own cheat sheet of examples and analogies that pertain to your industry and use that in your content.

RULE #3 - Create the content and be consistent
So now that you have determined who the content is for, come up with a content strategy and have gathered stories, analogies, data and/or examples to illustrate the point of your content, it is time to create it.

I believe in taking imperfect action.

The rough draft of this book is terrible as I write this in November of 2020. But if I get hung up on how terrible it is, this book will not exist.

I encounter many people who want to create content but who are held up for some reason by an impossible standard they feel they need to meet.

If you don't start creating, you will not know what works and what doesn't.

One of the problems that plagues business owners and content creators is staying consistent with their content creation.

Here are some tips to help with that.

Plan your content ahead of time. While you could get inspired to create a piece of content, realize that inspiration is fickle. So relying on serendipitous "inspiration" is not a plan.

Where possible, plan your content a week or at least a month in advance.

Here's how this works.

Let's say you decide to create one YouTube video per week. That means that in a month, you will need to release 4 videos on your channel.

Using the methods we'll discuss in Chapter 6, come up with the topics for those 4 videos at the beginning of the month.

In my case, because I am so active on YouTube, I will then write down three to five ideas that I want to discuss in each video.

So for instance, if I choose to do a video on "how to get freelance writing clients next week", I will sit down and write at least three ideas I want to share in the video. This gives me an outline of what I want to discuss for the video.

I used to fully script my videos so I would not fumble on my words. I don't do that as much any more because I have gotten enough practice to not fumble as much.

Once you have the four video ideas and you have written down the points you want to hit in each of those videos, it is time to record them!

I love to batch-create my content.

This just means, you pick a day or two to create all your content at once.

Batch creating will save you so many headaches!

In my case, since I am a video girl, I will do my make-up and plan to record 3 or 4 videos in one day.

Since I am on video, all I do sometimes is change the shirt I am wearing and all of a sudden it's like I am filming the video on a different day!

Anyway, once you have batch-created your content, you can then take the time to edit the videos or in my case, I drop them in Google Drive and allow my awesome video editor Brian to get to work on them. Last but not least, once the videos are edited, I will upload them to YouTube and then schedule them to go out each week so I don't miss a week.

This is the secret to the consistency of most content creators I know. And you can do this for any type of content and on any platform.

Plan ahead and batch-create yourself to content greatness.

Now, here's another word about consistency - you get to define what consistency means to you.

Personally, I think when it comes to your main content platform like a blog, podcast or YouTube channel where you post longer form content, one piece of content per week is enough for you to stay top of mind.

For secondary, short-form platforms like Instagram or Twitter, daily posts are in order.

Posting consistently in this way builds your authority and will keep you top of mind for the people who are silently following and waiting for their chance to work with you or patronize your business.

Here's another thing to think about.

Let's say you visit an online business and want to learn more about them. You search their website and find that they have a blog.

"Ohh exciting", you say to yourself because perhaps you assume that their blog will give you more information about what they do and how they can help you.

You click over to their blog and find out that the blog has not been updated since October of 2019. Then you notice they have an Instagram account, and so you decide to check them out on there.

The problem? They have only 10 posts on Instagram and their last post is from two months ago.

And they have a Twitter account that still has the generic egg icon that Twitter gives you when you sign up for an account.

Compare that with an online business that puts out one blog post per week that answers questions you have as a potential customer. In addition, they post three times per week to their Instagram account.

Which business are you likely to pick up the phone and call?

It is important to realize as a business owner that we live in a completely new economy. A majority of individuals under the age of 40 will be checking for your social media presence and reviews, before they ever contact your business to work with you. So if you are lax about that, you are literally losing money.

RULE #4 - Grab their attention
Not all content is created equal.

Some people seem to be able to generate a lot of activity and action around their content. While for others, everything seems flat.

Now, I know that likes, comments and followers do not pay the bills.

That is not what I am talking about here.

If you want your content to reach your intended audience, it is important that your content grabs *their* attention.

You want people to read your blog posts, listen to your podcast, watch your videos and engage your social media posts so that you can reach the folks who will buy from you.

But you cannot do that, until you grab their attention.

So how do you do that?

This is where you, my dear content creator friend, will need to learn the art of persuasive language.

Many books have been written on persuasion and I know persuasion is always an area I am always growing in.

Before I share some key tips to get you started on the path to becoming persuasive, it is important to understand that persuasion is not the same as trickery.

Yes, con men can use these same principles to trick people or win their confidence (hence the name "confidence man"). However, you can use these tips and be genuine in your selling.

TIPS ON PERSUASION

To persuade someone, you need to understand them.
There is an old adage that says "you can't understand someone until you have walked a mile in their shoes".

I agree.

I am an African.

My hair is tightly coiled into what is described as a 4C texture. It will be hard for me to take advice from someone who does not have 4C hair or who has not worked extensively with people with 4C hair on how to take proper care of my hair.

You're able to persuade people more when you show that you "get" them. You must show that you understand your audience's needs if you'll ever persuade them.

The first step to doing this of course is what we talked about earlier - understanding the demographics and psychographics of the people you serve with your business.

- What keeps them up at night?
- What scares them?
- What is that pain they would do anything to solve?
- How do they feel when they are going through that pain?
- What books do they read? What TV shows do they watch? Which conferences do they attend?
- Is there a language that is peculiar to this group? For instance, almost every graduate student understands what a thesis is and why p-values matter.

It is important as a business owner who wants to create content that sizzles and sells to understand these things about your audience.

You are more likely to persuade people when you speak their

language.

As sales copywriting expert Dan Kennedy puts it "crawl inside their minds and hearts".

After you have crawled into the hearts and minds of your audience or potential clients and customers, **ask yourself if your content serves *them*.**

This is where you'll have to be brutally honest with yourself.

Is the content you're putting out speaking their language? Is it drawing them in?

Is it showing them that you *get them* and that *you're* the best choice to solve their problem?

If your content doesn't answer these questions, I would think twice about putting it out.

Whatever content you create, think about how your relationship with potential buyers could grow further and lead them to patronize your business.

And even for those who only stick around for the free content, creating the kind of content that speaks to them has the potential to make them fans and walking billboards for your business.

Be compelling at the beginning.

You can know your audience inside out and create the best content for them, but if the presentation of your content is not catchy and compelling, you can forget it.

Contrary to the popular saying, people do in fact judge a book by its cover.

If you write blog posts, your titles matter.

On YouTube, titles and thumbnails are what get you the click throughs so people watch.

On Instagram, the first line of your caption better be compelling!

Grabbing attention starts the moment people encounter your content and skim the first thing they see about it.

Thus, it is important to make these compelling.

There are a number of tools out there that will help you with writing compelling headlines.

Here are a few online tools to help you create compelling and powerful content that draws people in.

Smart Blogger's 801+ Power Words That Pack A Punch and Convert Like Crazy -
https://smartblogger.com/power-words/

This is a massive list of over 800 words that make your words more compelling. It doesn't matter if you use them in blog posts, Instagram posts or in videos. These words work and you will be better for using them!

These words are powerful because they spark emotions. Used

right, your content will indeed convert casual browsers to buyers like crazy.

CoSchedule Headline Analyzer

The CoSchedule Headline Analyzer will analyze your headlines and give you a score based on the length of the headline, the power words you have used in the headline and on the psychology of how people skim headlines when they read.

Remember, you are going to draw someone into your content by the title on your YouTube video, podcast or blog post. The first line of your Facebook, Twitter or Instagram post matters.

This tool makes it easier for you to write great headlines.

Robert W. Bly's book *Words That Sell* is also a good book to delve into if you want to incorporate powerful words into your content.

Hint: There are several tools out there to help you take your content from bland to brilliant. I try to focus on a few so I am not overwhelmed but yet still create content that catches the eye and draws people in. The three I have suggested will give you an excellent launchpad. But don't stop there! Always be looking to improve the way you present your content. This is how you continue to grow your brand and influence through content.

Deliver on the promise you made in the beginning.

Now that you got their attention, it is important to keep it.

You have written a killer headline with all the powerful words and proper psychology.

Don't leave the person who is consuming your content hanging! It is now time to make good on your promise.

And the way you do that is to give them exactly what you advertised. If you said they would learn five ways to sew a dress even if you're a beginner, please give them that. Don't write that headline and then give them one way to sew and tell them to buy your eBook to learn the other four.

That's deceptive and it will make people lose trust in you.

It is important to understand that in a given day, there are thousands of stimuli vying for your ideal client's or customer's attention.

If you do this more than once, that person will lose interest in you and will find someone else they think is more honest.

So please, use everything you have learned so far to create the exact content they came to you for.

RULE #5 - Provide a call to action
Back in the day, I would create content without a call-to-action and wonder why nobody was buying my eBooks or asking about my services as a coach or writer.

Hello!

It was because even though I had created fantastic content, I had not given them a ***call-to-action***. Once you have grabbed their attention and gotten them to consume that piece of content, you must give people a call-to-action.

There is strong research however that shows that if you give a call-to-action, you increase the chances that somebody takes that action than if you don't. If you want people to call your business, include that call-to-action in your content.

If you need more reviews for your podcast or you are a local business that needs more reviews on Yelp or Google, ask people to do that.

As a business owner and content creator, you should never assume that people will "figure this out" on their own. Even the smartest and most well-intentioned people will forget about things if you don't ask directly or remind them.

A call-to-action can take several forms.

Here are a few examples you can use online.

- Call us NOW.
- Click here to purchase.
- Click the link to watch the video.
- Click the link to read the blog post
- Enter your name below to download the free eBook
- Buy this NOW
- Become an insider now
- Book your stay with us today

- Email us right now
- Send a text to...

Whatever the action is, spell it out. Never assume people will automatically take the action.

Which brings me to an important point.

In planning your content, it is important to also decide beforehand what action you would want consumers/potential clients/customers to take.

This should be built into your planning so that when you do post content, you include the relevant calls-to-action.

For instance, if you know that during a particular month, your business will be launching a new product or providing a sale on a product or service, it is important to note this on your content calendar and strategically weave it into your content.

When you're intentional with your content this way, you are bound to see more of the results you want.

CHAPTER 6

12 WAYS GENERATE CONTENT IDEAS THAT SIZZLE AND SELL

In order to stay consistent with content, you have to have content ideas.

So now how do we find content ideas to create?

In this chapter, you are going to learn about all the delightful ways to find content ideas so you never run out!

But the freest and most accessible tool of all is to *ask the people you are creating content for.*

Now, I'll admit that this is hard!

When I first started blogging, every blog post I read would say "ask your audience". But then what if you don't have an audience and you're starting from scratch? What if you ask and only one person gives you a response?

Well, personally, I think even if all you have is 20 people, you should still ask them.

Yes, you might only get one or two responses back, but that

information is gold. It gives you insight into what the other people who did not answer but who have been lurking around and consuming your content are thinking.

Which brings me to a mini-lesson I want to pause and share here. There are a lot of people who consume what you create who will never talk back to you online.

They will not comment. They will not hit the like button. They might not even share what you create. But let me tell you this: they are the ones who are watching you closely to see if you're legit and if they should spend their money with you.

So when you're creating content, you are creating it for both types of people - the individuals who engage like crazy as well as the lurkers.

So don't be afraid to ask.

That being said, the online tools I share below will allow you to research and discover content ideas even if your audience is small or you have nobody to ask. Most of these are paid tools but they have limited free versions. Usually, the free versions will suffice but if you intend on making content an integral marketing piece for your business, I would recommend paying for one or two of them.

Below, I will discuss ten of the tools I've found the most useful in my 7-year content creation and marketing journey.

Answer The Public

Answer The Public is a tool that allows you to research the exact phrases and questions being put into search engines like Google.

When you have a small audience or no audience, using Answer The Public is your way of "cheating" and finding out what the people who will potentially become your audience members are looking for.

Type in the keyword you would like to create content around.

Once you do that, Answer The Public will spit out questions that people are asking in search engines.

Once the questions come up, you are able to download them as a CSV file. A CSV file is similar to an Excel Spreadsheet and so you will already have them neatly organized.

You now have a nicely organized list of questions your audience can find you for.

Now here's the kicker: each question on that list is a piece of content you create an answer for.

And in answering those questions, you will begin to establish yourself as an authority for those who are looking for the solution you provide in your business.

Exploding Topics

Exploding Topics is a tool that helps you discover topics that are popular and trending. While I absolutely hate following trends, there is something powerful about them.

If you are able to catch the right trend at the right time, it could do massive wonders for your business.

A mentor of mine calls this "trend-surfing".

In the sport of surfing, surfers wait to catch the right wave before they get on their boards.

You can do the same with your content.

For instance, I am writing this book as part of NaNoWriMo 2020. NaNoWrimo is the National Novel Writing Month that happens in November every year. Each year, authors set a goal to write 50,000 words towards a novel in the month of November.

Now, clearly, this is not a novel.

And if you took the time to count the words in here, you will notice that I have less than 50,000 words!

But because this is a popular trend that happens each November amongst writers and authors, I took advantage of that fact and started a live writing sprint series on my YouTube channel that went on for 14 days in November 2020.

Because I was creating content around a popular subject, people found me and came to my writing sessions who had never encountered me. It also helped that the YouTube algorithm was pushing my videos towards new viewers.

Thus, I recommend that you stay abreast with general and niche-specific trends.

I remember when mega-star Rihanna's beauty line Fenty Beauty came out in 2017, all the beauty influencers on Instagram and YouTube were scrambling to be the first to create content on this.

A lot of them can attribute the growth of their brands around that time to creating video tutorials on the various looks you could achieve with Fenty Beauty make-up.

Creating content around trends can pour fuel on what you're doing. Here's my word of caution however - don't create content exclusively around trends. People will get tired of it, see you as an "opportunist" and not the authority you are.

Ride the wave, but do it sensibly.

Google Autosuggest
Google Autosuggest is one of the most under-utilized tools for content creation in my opinion.

All you need to do is to start typing something into Google (you can do this on YouTube as well) and Google will begin to "auto-suggest" the other similar ways people search for what you are typing in.

Once you have typed in your key phrase and hit "search", and you scroll to the bottom of the search page, you will find phrases related to the one you just searched. These are opportunities for content that Google, the biggest search engine on the planet, is offering to you for free.

Ubersuggest

I have used Ubersuggest to greatly increase blog traffic for my clients and I am happy to recommend it to you.

This tool allows you to research the keywords that competitor websites are ranking in search engines for.

It also gives you the volume of people searching for a term in Google.

In addition, you can learn about the "SEO difficulty" for a keyword or phrase. This indicates how difficult or not it would be to get a blog post you have written to show up on the first page of Google.

SEO for bloggers is more in depth than anything I can cover in this book - and it is ever-evolving. But, I can assure you, that if you intend on being found in search engines for written content, Ubersuggest is an excellent place for you to start.

Watch this tutorial on how to use Ubersuggest.
https://youtu.be/Ch_4Gajeih4

Buzzsumo

Buzzsumo is not free. But you can try the software for 30 days which is usually enough time to collect a lot of data.

Buzzsumo gives you information on a number of things but the two below are what I like to focus on.

1. How many times a piece of written content has been shared on social media. If you see how much a post has been shared on social media, it gives you an idea of content that is popular and which will do well once you've created it. You get to see how popular a post is on Facebook, Twitter, Reddit and Pinterest.

2. You also get insights on the backlinks a piece of written content has received. A backlink happens when another blog or website links back to your blog or website.

Backlinks are powerful in the eyes of Google. The more backlinks a website has, the more authority it has in the eyes of Google and as such the more likely it is for Google to surface that content to the top of their search engine. Thus, if you plan on blogging as part of your content strategy, getting backlinks to your blog should be something you focus on.

Buzzsumo gives you the links to websites that have linked back to a particular blog post or website.

This is important to know because by knowing the websites that have sent backlinks to websites similar to yours, you can use that information to reach out to those websites to get backlinks as well.

A word of caution here.

I have been a blogger and content creator long enough to know that some people abuse this information.

Four to five times each month, I will receive an email from someone I have never heard of or met, that asks me to place a link to their blog or website (some I have never heard of before) on my blog.

Most of the emails go like this:

"We read your blog and think it is wonderful. In fact, we were hoping that you could link to our newly published post on our website that talks about fly-fishing in Alaska. Would you be willing to link to it on your website?"

Here are a few reasons why I immediately delete these types of emails.

First of all, it is likely they have never read my blog. In fact, sometimes I will get pitches like these that have absolutely nothing to do with the niche that I write in. It is a dead give away that they have not taken the time (nor do they care) to read my blog.

Secondly, when you ask someone to do something for you without a relationship and out of context, those individuals are likely to decline. It's called the law of reciprocity. While I am not saying you should only do things for people who do something for you, sending this type of request is selfish on the part of the person who is seeking the link.

I believe in offering value first, before you ask for anything. If you want someone to do something for you, make it worth their time.

Instead of spamming inboxes with these types of emails, here are 3 powerful ways to get links instead.

- Work on building relationships with bloggers and writers for publications that you would like to receive links on. People are more likely to do something like that for you when they realize you're genuine. And in fact, this is general good advice! Build real relationships with people where you can offer some kind of value *first, before* you ask for anything.
- One of the ways I like to indirectly get links back to my website is by being a podcast interview guest. When you appear as a guest on a podcast, every good podcast host will create show notes for the interview. When they do, they will typically ask for links to your website. And just like that, you have a backlink. I find this way of getting backlinks great because it is a win-win situation. The podcast host gets content for their podcast. And the guest is able to market their business to a new audience as well as get a backlink to their blog/website that helps them in search engines.
- Use Help A Reporter Out. Help A Reporter Out or HARO is a website where writers and journalists

go to find subject-matter experts to comment on a topic. You can sign up to get daily requests of this sort. Once you receive the email alerts, you can browse through and find which ones suit you and answer the query. In a lot of cases, these writers/journalists will ask for a link to your website and there again is another opportunity to receive a backlink.

Soovle

When you go on Soovle.com it is built similarly to any search engine you will encounter on the internet.

The unique thing about Soovle however is that when you type in a keyword, the top keywords and key phrases for that subject on different platforms like YouTube, Amazon and Google will show up.

Amazon Kindle

People are always shocked when I mention Amazon Kindle as a place to get content ideas. And no, you don't need to buy anything.

Here's how to use Amazon to find ideas to create on.

Go into the Amazon Kindle store and search for a topic. Once you've done that, enter a keyword or key phrase and look at the top 5 results or best-selling books that come up.

Once you find at least 5 of these books, use the "Look Inside" feature to look at the table of contents.

The titles for each of the chapters in the table of contents can spark some incredible ideas for your content creation process!

Quora.com

Quora.com is a popular question and answer website where I have found incredible questions to answer on my YouTube channel and blog.

If you're an expert in a subject, you can begin answering questions there daily to build your authority as well.

Plus, when you provide insightful answers to questions on Quora, it can lead to traffic to your own platform.

TubeBuddy/VidIQ

If you plan to create video content on YouTube, TubeBuddy and VidIQ are a must. Both are keyword research tools that are more nuanced that I can describe in this book.

And they are the reason I've been able to consistently grow my YouTube channel since 2017.

Pinterest Trends

Pinterest Trends tells you what people are actively searching for on Pinterest in a given period.

I am writing the first edition of this book in November of 2020. In the United States, the third Thursday of November marks Thanksgiving.

So guess what's trending on Pinterest trends? Thanksgiving recipes.

If you were a food blogger, this would definitely be your time to create some yummy Thanksgiving recipes you could share on Pinterest and receive attention for.

Be inspired by other people's work
This doesn't mean you should steal other people's work. Don't do that. However, I love that there are content creators who have gone ahead of me and are prolific at creating content. When I started on YouTube for instance, I would go to YouTube channels that I thought I would share an audience with and would search for their most popular video.

You can do this by navigating to the VIDEOS tab on a YouTube channel and then by filtering their videos by most popular.

If you use a tool like VidIQ on YouTube for instance, you would be able to tell the "velocity" on the video. This refers to how many people are watching those popular videos per hour.

A video may be popular, but is anyone still watching it?

VidIQ helps you answer that question.

Once I would come up with a list of videos that I thought would fit my channel, I would put my own spin on it and create that video.

To date, some of those videos are my best-performing. A video I did on how to share your YouTube channel on Instagram stories using an Android has now garnered over 77,000 views. I used the exact method above to come up with the idea!

So don't be afraid to be inspired by what others are creating.

**Look in the comments section*
Listen to me when I tell you that the comments section of any post you encounter online is pure gold!

This is especially true on large accounts online that may not have time to answer every comment.

If you scan those comments you will find real questions that real people are asking.

This is your chance!

Answer those questions with your content.

Look at your analytics
Last but definitely not least, don't ignore your own analytics.

Every platform you create content on has some sort of in-built analytics that you can check out.

Don't ignore these.

There's a popular phrase that says, "what gets measured, gets improved."

How do you know if your content is reaching people? How

do you know it is reaching the right people?

You know it by your analytics.

And so, I encourage you to check out your analytics at least once a month for a few reasons:

- You will see your content pieces that performed the best and be able to create more content along those lines.
- You will also find out which content pieces received the least response.
- When you are looking at analytics, you are not just looking at likes, comments and shares. You are also looking at how well that content converted. Which is the topic of the next chapter.

CHAPTER 7

MEASURE YOUR CONTENT SUCCESS

So now you're answering all these questions on the internet and getting found because you are doing it so well.

How do you know when that content has worked for you and your brand?

You will know when people begin to buy from you.

If you're a business however, then your content should sell for you. I don't care who says what, your content should ultimately sell what you are selling.

In general, there is usually a progression to this and you should have goals for each of these.

Awareness
The first step is making people aware of your content and ultimately what you have to offer.

Unless it is an emergency, most people do their research before they decide to purchase anything.

This is why they people go and read reviews on Yelp. This is why they will text friends and family who have used a service to ask what their experience was.

People will go online and find out if you have a website or some kind of social presence.

Before someone buys from you, they usually have done their homework.

This makes it all the more critical for businesses today to be intentional about creating content.

When people find your content, it is a powerful way for you to introduce your business to them, tell them what you stand for and how you can solve their problems.

People will become aware *of* you through your content.

Engagement
Another metric to measure is the engagement rate on your content. Now, for me, this metric is a vanity metric.

You cannot take likes and comments to the bank.

I wish likes and comments on my social media posts paid the bills! I would be rich!

However, increased engagement helps with algorithms and extending your reach. Here's what I mean.

Every social media platform depends on algorithms.

Software engineers build programs embedded in these platforms that take many factors into account when it comes to promoting specific pieces of content to a broader audience.

For instance, on YouTube, engagement on your video is a big deal.

YouTube measures engagement by how many people have clicked through a thumbnail to watch a video, how long those people stayed after they clicked through, the comments, likes and dislikes that a video gets.

Based on these signals, YouTube will promote that piece of content to a wider audience beyond your subscribers.

And in doing so, you are discovered by some who never knew you existed and are able to bring in new leads for your business.

Thus, even though likes and comments and engagement will not pay you directly, it can eventually pay you if you are strategic about it and use the tips I've shared so far in this book to create engaging content for the right audience.

Thus, regardless of the content you're creating, it is important to measure engagement in the form of:

- Blog traffic
- Podcast downloads
- Video views
- Likes
- Comments
- Shares

Apart from platform algorithms favoring content that is getting high engagement, when more people engage with your content, it is a form of social proof.

I first encountered the idea of social proof in the book *Influence*, by Robert Cialdini.

Social proof is the idea that when we see *other* people doing something, we are more likely to do it also.

If you see that 1 million people have viewed a video, it will make you wonder "Huh! Let me see why 1 million people have watched this video".

On the other hand, if you see a video that has about 10 views, even though that video may be better than the one that has garnered a million, we quickly assume that the video must not be good and it will take a little more convincing for us to commit to watching that video.

It's a natural human response.

Social proof is important when you're creating content.

Now of course, if you are brand new to content, you may not have the social proof just yet.

This is normal. Don't beat yourself up over it and do not quit because of it!

Over time, as you create the right content for the right audience, you will in fact build that social proof.

And yes, social proof can grow your business because it communicates authority and trust. People are more likely to buy from someone they deem an authority and someone they trust.

Clicks to website/landing page

Another metric you can track is how many people come to your website or to a specific landing page from other content platforms.

If you are a business with a website, this metric should be important to you if you would like to estimate or calculate your conversion rate. A conversion rate looks at the people who took an action - whether that action was to buy a product, book an appointment or sign up for an email freebie after they have clicked through and landed on a specific page of your website.

For the math enthusiasts out there, this is how you would calculate the conversion rate:

The number of people who took the desired action divided by Number of people who visited the website landing page) multiplied by 100.

This calculation will give you a percentage.

In the world of online marketing, a conversion rate of 2% is considered standard

This means, in general, 2 out of 100 contacts or leads you generate will take the action you want them to.

I tend to use it as a benchmark too but please don't be limited by it!

Personally, I think if you have done a great job of reaching the right people with the right content, you could convert well above that.

Sales

This is the part we all want to get to.

To make a sale as a result of the content we've created. We have not gone through ALL of this work just to entertain folks. Your content should be tied to your profit goal as well. Thus, you can also measure the effectiveness of your content by looking at the sales it brings it.

And sales will look different for everyone.

- For coaches, is your content getting people to inquire more about your coaching?
- For authors, is your content selling more of your books?
- If you are a hairstylist, is it getting you more bookings?

Your content should ultimately get you more sales. It should make more people want to work with you. If your content is not helping you make more sales, you need to re-evaluate what you're doing.

Again, this is where call-to-actions become important. If you are not putting your services out there in your content and you are not making calls for people to buy from you, don't assume people will.

I've been online long enough to know that with everything else being equal, the person who gives more frequent calls-to-action is the one who gets more business. So don't be shy.

Ask, ask and ask some more!

CHAPTER 8

REPURPOSING YOUR CONTENT

There is no need to reinvent the wheel.

One of the reasons people stop in their tracks when it comes to creating content is because they come to a place where they *think* they have run out of content ideas.

The truth however is akin to the first law of thermodynamics in physics that states, "the energy in a system is neither created nor destroyed; it is simply converted from one form to another."

This is absolutely true for content as well!

Good content is never really "created" nor "destroyed". It is simply converted from one form to another. You don't have to create something new from scratch each and every time you decide to create content. You are absolutely free to repurpose your content. In this chapter, we'll talk about repurposing your content like a pro so you're not stressing yourself each time.

Why should you repurpose your content?

First of all, it saves you time.

Secondly, the people that saw that piece of content the first time will not be the exact same people who see it the next time. Especially if you are repurposing six to twelve months after it was posted the first time.

So don't be afraid to do this.

Here are 5 ways to repurpose your content like the profession you are!

Use the same post again

So here's the thing, as you continue to grow your content online, the number of people that follow you will grow.

If you made a post 6 months ago which was consumed by 100 people for instance, there are still people who never saw that piece of content.

It is perfectly fine to re-post that piece of content (with a few tweaks) and create something new.

For a blogger, this might mean that you revamp your top blog posts each year and repost them.

For someone who creates on Instagram, this could mean using the same caption as you did 6 months ago because there are brand new folks who have not heard of you yet.

Will you have people say "oh, this is a re-post"? Yes, you might.

But we don't care about other people's opinions. We care about content that helps us convert casual browsers into buyers. So we don't worry about the detractors who think it is their business to point this out. Never feel guilty about reposting the same content - especially if it worked before.

Take a larger piece of content and "chop" it up"
You can also take a larger piece of content, break it up into tiny bites and serve it up as delicious snacks of content. This is especially useful for your longer form content like YouTube videos, podcast episodes and blog posts. For your blog posts, you can pull quotes, tips and highlights and create graphics using a tool like Canva or Typorama.

For YouTube videos, you can use a tool like Headliner to create a 30-60 second snippet that you can share to your social media platforms. Headliner allows you to do the same thing to podcast episodes.

You can create as many or as few of these as you want and use them on whichever platform you want to use them on.

Do a mash-up of your best content
If you have even 10 pieces of content, there are ideas, thoughts and concepts that will be the "best of".

You can take these "best of" ideas and create a new content piece out of that.

This is exactly how people come up with "top 10" lists for instance.

Turn your content into a book

Can I tell you a little secret?

This book you're reading right now, was born out of the content I wrote on my blog MyOnlineBizJourney.com for 5 years.

I have updated a lot of the points I discussed on that blog for the era we live in. But most of the ideas came from the original content I wrote on that blog.

Again, you are reading this book and it is fresh for you because when I first wrote that content, you did not read it.But now, I've presented it in book format and here you are enjoying it.

Michael Hyatt's book *Platform*, is a book that took the ideas on his blog for leaders on how to build a platform online.

You can do the same thing.

Turn your content into a different format
You can turn a blog post into a video.

You can transcribe that podcast and turn it into a blog post or part of an email newsletter.

Lumen5 is a tool that allows you to turn your blog posts into videos.

My goal here is to get you to see that you don't have to scramble to create new content all the time.

You can turn points in your blog posts into Instagram stories.

If you created that content, it is your right (and maybe even your responsibility) to take that piece and revamp it into something fresh!

CHAPTER 9

EXPANDING YOUR REACH

As a creative business owner, you want to be able to expand your reach so you can find potential new clients all the time.

Here is the reality: in most of the cases we have discussed so far, you are going to be at the mercy of a tech giant's algorithm.

YouTube has an algorithm that can be hard to crack. Instagram is constantly changing how it chooses to surface content to the people that follow you. Twitter is super crazy fast and so if people are not intentionally looking out for your tweets, most of them will go unnoticed. Google tweaks the rules for ranking in their search engine each year.

So how is a person supposed to win when you constantly have to learn what the new rules are?

I know.

I get frustrated too.

But as you have seen so far, this is not a reason not to create content.

There is still a lot of potential for people to find your content, engage with it and ultimately become buyers in your business.

In fact, it is possible that you will create a piece of content that goes wildly viral and all of a sudden, you rise from obscurity to popularity - with the right people finding you and your offers. Depending solely on some algorithm however is not a smart idea. And in fact, depending on virality is not necessarily a smart marketing move, either.

There are famous examples of companies that have gone viral - for the wrong reasons - and it has hurt them rather than be a blessing.

You can go viral and still be broke. Always remember this.

One thing that can absolutely help you beat any algorithm is to expand your reach by collaborating with other people in your space.

Here is the deal - there are people, who are currently serving your audience.

There are individuals who are serving sub-sections and cross-sections of your ideal audience.

If they are actively creating content online, *they are not your competition.*

Let me repeat that last part of the sentence.

These folks are not your competition.

They are people to collaborate with and it is important to see it as such. Let me give you a few examples from my own experience.

From podcast guest to booking coaching clients.

I was a podcast guest on a podcast in early 2019. The podcast is targeted towards nurses who want to turn their knowledge into a business. On this show, I talked about how I started my writing and blogging business and how that had paid off in so many ways for me and my family.

There were individuals who found me from the show and started following me online.

I continued to show up with my content.

Within a month of that podcast going live, someone who found me on the show booked my 3-hour intensive 1:1 session for writers that cost $497 at the time.

It did not end there.

Another listener of the podcast would later book me for a 1:1 coaching session for $697 so I could help her complete her first book.

All from being a guest on a podcast for 30 or 40 minutes.

Later on, the host of that podcast brought me on to teach a cohort of 10 women how to write their books and paid me a healthy four-figure amount to do so.

YouTube channel mention gets me a client

In this instance, I didn't even collaborate with this individual. I just happened to be one of their live videos on YouTube.

I was just hanging out like everyone else supporting her work. And then, I made a comment that caused the host of the live video to mention my name. The following week, I had someone booking my 1:1 $497 3-hour intensive!

Listen, the power of collaboration is wild!

How to expand your reach through collaborations

So now, let's talk about how you can expand your reach by collaborating with other business owners/content creators.

#1 Build your own platform first

This seems obvious but let me mention this here.

If you want to collaborate with other business owners and content creators who have already built an audience you would like to introduce yourself to, it is important to build your platform first.

You don't need thousands of followers. And you don't need to have created content for the last ten years.

But there should be something you can refer to.

Let me illustrate with an example.

In October of 2020, I received an email from an individual

who wanted me to be a guest on their upcoming online summit. If you are not aware of what an online summit is, it is a type of online conference where several speakers speak on a central theme.

Although they are not as popular as they used to be between 2012 and 2015, they are still around and can be a lucrative way to build an audience while collaborating with other creators in the niche or space.

Well, I received the email with very little context and no much more than, "Can you come and speak at my online summit?"

I am not a callous person.

I try to respond to people who email me when I feel the request is genuine.

But with an increasingly busy schedule, it has become difficult to do this realistically without burning out.

Anyway, I decided to check this individual out.

I clicked on the link to their website that was in the signature.

The blog had 7 posts.

The last one had been written in March of 2020 - 7 months before she was reaching out to me to collaborate with her on her online summit.

I reached out and mentioned this fact and asked her if I could see any other work she had online before I would agree to anything. I got a few responses back with some excuses and a promise that once her assistant finished the page for the summit, she would send it to me. I am writing this at the end of November 2020, I still have not heard back from this person.

I didn't even give them an outright "no" - something that I know larger creators would have probably done.

I just asked them to show me proof of their work before I could agree to collaborating with her.

When you have not built your platform before you reach out to collaborate with someone else who has spent years, money and time to build up their brand and audience, here is what that looks like.

1. It looks like you are not serious. You may in fact be serious, but if the last time you wrote a blog post was six months ago and they cannot find any other evidence of your content online, I can 100% assure you that the person you want to collaborate with will pass.
2. Every creator wants to align themselves with successful people. This sounds snooty - I know. But it is the way the world works. If the quality of your content is poor, you are not consistent and there is strong evidence that you have not put the work in to build your brand, the other creator will pass. This has less to do with how many followers you have and

more to do with the quality of your work even though you might be a smaller content creator.

If you have a clear message and you are a consistent content creator serving up the kind of content that answers the questions in your audience, it is likely that people will collaborate with you.

So take your time to build your platform.

#2- Be a person of value

What are you bringing to the table? Every time I reach out to be a guest on a podcast or collaborate with someone, I lead with what I can offer them first.

This will require a bit of research on your part. If you plan on collaborating with another YouTube creator for instance, what type of content have you noticed will be valuable to them that they have not created yet? Yes, this takes a bit of time but once you find that content gap, you can pitch yourself and if the other person feels the same, trust me, they will be happy to collaborate with you.

#3 - Look for content creators around your level of growth

While I am all about shooting your shot with creators and business owners who are far bigger than you, I find that it is easier to connect with creators around my level or just a bit above that who also have dedicated audiences. In fact, I find that I've converted better when I have collaborated with these smaller, niche creators. So look for people who are still growing and build relationships with those people.

CHAPTER 10

THE REAL SECRET SAUCE TO SIZZLING CONTENT THAT SELLS

Last but not least, I want to leave you with this: you are the secret sauce.

I don't care how many people are doing the same thing you are, YOU ARE THE SECRET SAUCE of your content.

Pump your personality, your quirks, your accent, your stories and everything that is you into your content.

People might find you because of an algorithm or because they listened to you on someone's podcast. But they will stick around and interact with you because they fall in love with your personality. So let it shine. You don't have to bare everything but let them see *you*.

If you've enjoyed this book and received value from it, it would be my honor to receive a review of this book you just read on Amazon so other people can find this book as well.

Other books by Gertrude Nonterah on Amazon

Win At Freelance Writing

www.ingramcontent.com/pod-product-compliance
Lightning Source LLC
Chambersburg PA
CBHW070941210326
41520CB00021B/7002